AF480678

THE POWER OF APPRECIATION

HOW GRATITUDE CAN TRANSFORM YOUR RELATIONSHIPS

DR. MINAKSHI BANSAL

DEDICATION

This book is dedicated to all those who strive to find light in the small moments, who cherish the warmth of a simple "thank you," and who believe in the transformative power of kindness and appreciation. To my family and friends, whose unwavering support and love remind me every day of the incredible strength that lies in our connections with one another. And to you, the reader, who has embarked on this journey to deepen your relationships through gratitude—may you find joy and fulfillment in every grateful moment.

ᗐᗐᗐ

Contents

Contents

Prayer

"Om Bhadram Karnebhih Shrinuyama Devah
Bhadram Pashyemakshabhiryajatrah
Sthirairangais Tushtuvamsastanubhih
Vyashema Devahitam Yadayuh
Svasti Na Indro Vriddhashravah
Svasti Nah Pusha Vishwavedah
Svasti Nastarkshyo Arishtanemih
Svasti No Brihaspatir Dadhatu
Om Shantih Shantih Shantih"

This mantra is a prayer for universal well-being, invoking the blessings of various deities for protection, health, and happiness. It emphasizes the importance of experiencing the auspicious through all senses and living a life aligned with divine purpose. The repetition of "Shantih" at the end signifies a deep desire for peace in the individual, the environment, and the universe at large. This mantra is often recited as a prayer for peace, prosperity, and the physical and spiritual well-being of all beings.

ᐅᐅᐅ

About The Author

Dr. Minakshi Bansal, born in the bustling metropolis of Delhi, India, has led a life steeped in artistry, scholarly pursuit, and an unwavering commitment to societal betterment. Following her marriage, she relocated to Ahmedabad, Gujarat, where she has since blossomed into a multifaceted beacon of inspiration for many. Dr. Minakshi is not only recognized as a gifted artist in the realm of Fine Arts but also as an esteemed author, a devoted social worker and a dedicated research scholar in Psychology. Her journey, marked by a profound dedication to elevating those around her, especially the downtrodden and underprivileged children of society, is a testament to her deep-seated belief in the transformative power of engagement and empathy.

From her earliest days, Minakshi was distinguished by an insatiable appetite for reading. Her literary universe was inhabited by characters and narratives that spanned ethical tales, motivational and inspirational stories, and the mythic parables imbued with life lessons. This voracious reading habit was not merely for personal edification but was driven by a desire to distill and disseminate the essence of these narratives to foster the development of students and peers alike. She was particularly captivated by the lives and teachings of historical figures and spiritual leaders such as Adi Shankaracharya, Swami Vivekananda, Dr. APJ Abdul Kalam, Mahamana Pandit Madan Mohan Malviya, Mahatma Gandhi, Sardar Vallabhai Patel, and Vinoba Bhave, among others. Their philosophies and life stories fueled her ambition to embody their ideals of resilience, selflessness, and relentless pursuit of knowledge.

Dr. Minakshi's academic and practical engagement with psychology has been equally noteworthy. As a research scholar, her focus has been on exploring the intricate tapestry of the human psyche, aiming to unlock the potential for psychological well-being and societal harmony. Her scholarly work is complemented by her active involvement in social work, where she employs her academic insights to make tangible differences in the lives of the underprivileged. Her endeavours in social work are characterized by an innovative approach that combines traditional wisdom with contemporary psychological practices to address the multifaceted challenges faced by these communities.

Her artistic talents, another facet of her diverse capabilities, are not merely a personal passion but also serve as a medium through which she communicates and connects with others. Her art, rich in symbolism and emotional depth, reflects her philosophical inquiries and social concerns, offering viewers a glimpse into the breadth of her intellect and the depth of her compassion.

In addition to her contributions to the arts and social sciences, Dr. Minakshi has embraced the healing arts of Pranic Healing, mastering the techniques developed by Master Choa Kok Sui. This practice, which focuses on the manipulation of Prana or life energy to heal the body and aura, has been both a personal journey of discovery and a means through which she extends her healing touch to others. Her proficiency in Pranic Healing is complemented by her advocacy and teaching of various forms of meditation aimed at rejuvenation, personal betterment, and the cultivation of harmony within individuals and communities alike.

Dr. Minakshi's life is a narrative of relentless pursuit, not just of personal achievement but of the upliftment and empowerment of society at large. Her diverse interests and talents—spanning the arts, literature, psychology, and the healing practices—converge on a singular path of service. She embodies the spirit of the luminaries who inspired her, channelling their legacy through her actions and teachings. Through her books, art, and social initiatives, she continues to inspire a new generation to embark on their own journeys of self-discovery, resilience, and altruism.

Her commitment to social betterment, particularly her focus on uplifting underprivileged children, reflects a deep understanding of the transformative potential of education and personal development. By integrating her knowledge of psychology, her artistic sensibilities, and her healing practices, Dr. Bansal has developed a holistic approach to social work that addresses both the immediate needs and the long-term well-being of the communities she serves.

As an author, Dr. Minakshi's writings offer a blend of inspirational insights, practical wisdom, and reflective contemplations drawn from her extensive reading and life experiences. Her books serve as a guide for those seeking to navigate the complexities of life with grace, resilience, and purpose. Through her narratives, she extends an invitation to her readers to explore the depths of their own potential and to contribute meaningfully to the collective well-being of society.

In Dr. Minakshi Bansal, we find a remarkable synthesis of the artist, the scholar, the healer, and the social activist. Her life's work stands as a beacon of hope and a source of inspiration for individuals seeking to make a difference in the world. Her story is a compelling reminder of the power of individual action, rooted in compassion and driven by a profound commitment to the betterment of humanity. Dr. Minakshi's legacy is not just in the tangible outcomes of her efforts but in the enduring spirit of inquiry, empathy, and service that she embodies.

ᚦᚦᚦ

Preface

In this book, we embark on a journey to explore a simple yet profound concept: gratitude. Often overlooked in the rush of everyday life, gratitude is a powerful force that can transform our relationships and enrich our interactions with others. Through the pages that follow, you will discover not just the importance of gratitude but also practical ways to incorporate it into your daily life, helping to foster deeper connections and enhance the quality of your interactions.

Gratitude is more than just saying thank you. It's a way of seeing the world, an attitude that acknowledges the good in our lives and recognizes the contributions of others. This recognition, when expressed genuinely, not only strengthens bonds but also builds trust and mutual respect. It creates a positive feedback loop in relationships, where kindness and appreciation lead to stronger connections and increased collaboration.

The power of gratitude extends beyond personal relationships. It influences professional interactions, community ties, and even our relationship with ourselves. In this book, I delve into the psychological and physiological benefits of gratitude, drawing on the latest research to show how this age-old virtue can lead to modern-day well-being and happiness. You will learn how gratitude can improve mental health, enhance physical health, and lead to a more fulfilling life.

Each chapter of this book provides insights into different aspects of gratitude—from its role in enhancing romantic relationships to its impact on workplace dynamics. You will find stories from real life, where the application of gratitude has brought about transformation and healing. These stories not only serve as proof of gratitude's effectiveness but also provide inspiration and hope.

Moreover, this book is designed to be interactive. I encourage you to not just read but also engage with the content through various suggested exercises and reflections. Whether it's starting a gratitude journal, creating a gratitude vision board, or simply integrating mindful moments of appreciation into your day, these practices are intended to make gratitude a living, breathing part of your everyday experience.

Importantly, the practice of gratitude requires consistency and commitment. It is not a quick fix but a lifelong journey. Like any other skill, gratitude becomes more profound and impactful with practice. This book aims to guide you on how to begin this practice and how to sustain it over time, transforming it from a simple exercise into a fundamental part of your life philosophy.

The benefits of gratitude are not limited to the person expressing it; they ripple out to affect everyone around them. By cultivating a grateful mindset, you contribute to a more positive and supportive environment wherever you go. This not only improves your life but also the lives of those around you, creating a cycle of positivity that can transform communities and societies.

As you turn the pages, I invite you to open your heart to the possibilities that gratitude holds. Allow the concepts and stories to challenge your current perceptions and inspire you to embrace gratitude more fully. This is not just about reading another self-help book; it's about embarking on a transformative journey that begins with recognizing the power of appreciation.

In closing, I hope that this book serves as both a guide and a companion as you explore the depths of gratitude. May you find within its pages the tools and inspiration needed to enrich your relationships and lead a more joyful, connected life. As you step forward into your journey of gratitude, remember that every moment of appreciation is a step towards a more fulfilled and meaningful existence.

Dr. Minakshi Bansal
Social Activist
Ahmedabad, Gujarat, Bharat

❦❦❦

ONE

INTRODUCTION TO APPRECIATION AND GRATITUDE

Appreciation and gratitude are cornerstone concepts in positive psychology, embodying the recognition and enjoyment of the good qualities of someone or something. Often considered as two sides of the same coin, these feelings play a crucial role in enhancing personal and collective well-being. While they are closely related, each carries a unique nuance: appreciation often implies an understanding, recognition, or admiration of value or quality, extending beyond mere possession or receipt of benefits. Gratitude, on the other hand, typically arises from the acknowledgment of a benefit received, whether tangible or intangible, from external sources.

The importance of gratitude and appreciation in everyday life cannot be overstated. They act as powerful catalysts for positive psychological change, influencing not just personal happiness but also profoundly impacting the quality of our relationships and interactions. When people regularly engage in the practice of recognizing and valuing the positive aspects of life and the contributions of others, they foster a more positive internal state and promote greater overall satisfaction in life.

One of the foundational theories that highlight the importance of gratitude is the "Broaden-and-Build" theory of positive emotions proposed by psychologist Barbara Fredrickson. This theory suggests that positive emotions broaden an individual's momentary thought-action repertoire, which in turn can build their personal resources, ranging from physical and intellectual resources to social and psychological ones. Gratitude, being a powerful positive emotion, contributes significantly to this broadening effect, helping individuals see beyond their immediate concerns and enhancing their coping mechanisms during challenging times.

Further emphasizing the transformative power of gratitude, research in neuroscience has shown that gratitude can lead to changes in brain function and structure. Studies using fMRI scans have demonstrated that expressing and experiencing gratitude activates the brain in areas associated with moral cognition, value judgment, and theory of mind. Moreover, this neural activity is associated with lasting emotional sensitivity to gratitude, suggesting that the more we practice gratitude, the more attuned we are to its emotional benefits.

In addition to its psychological and neurological benefits, gratitude also plays a vital role in social dynamics. It acts as a social glue, a way to strengthen existing relationships and foster new ones. When people express gratitude towards each other, they not only acknowledge the goodness in their lives but also recognize that the source of this goodness lies at least partially outside themselves. This recognition can build and enhance the social fabric of mutual support, creating deeper interpersonal connections and a sense of community.

However, understanding and practicing appreciation and gratitude are not always straightforward. In a fast-paced world, where negative news often dominates and personal ambitions can drive individuals toward relentless pursuit of more, taking the time to pause and reflect on what is already present and valuable can be challenging. The cultivation of gratitude requires a shift from what is lacking to what is abundant, from dissatisfaction to recognition of the sufficiency and richness of life's offerings.

To effectively integrate appreciation and gratitude into daily life, it is beneficial to engage in specific practices and rituals. Keeping a gratitude journal, where one regularly records things they are thankful for, can significantly increase awareness of positive experiences and enhance feelings of contentment. Similarly, expressing gratitude directly to others, whether through thank you notes, verbal acknowledgment, or thoughtful gestures, can strengthen relationships and enhance personal and collective happiness.

Moreover, it is essential to recognize that gratitude is not just a private but also a communal emotion. It has the potential to transcend individual experience, promoting greater societal well-being. By fostering an environment where appreciation is openly expressed and shared, communities can enhance resilience, deepen understanding, and encourage a more empathetic and supportive social climate.

The journey towards a grateful life is continuous and evolving. As individuals and societies, the pursuit of appreciation and gratitude is not merely about feeling better in the moment but about building a foundation for sustained emotional health and relational success. This pursuit, grounded in both ancient wisdom and modern science, holds the promise of transforming our relationships and crafting a more positive and interconnected world.

ᗞᗞᗞ

"Gratitude transforms the mundane into the extraordinary, revealing the beauty hidden in everyday encounters. It deepens our appreciation for the simple joys that often go unnoticed. Embrace gratitude, and watch your world transform."

♡♡♡

TWO

THE SCIENCE BEHIND GRATITUDE

The profound impact of gratitude on both the mind and body is well-documented through extensive psychological and physiological research. Gratitude, the feeling of thankfulness and appreciation for the tangible and intangible, affects individuals beyond mere emotional well-being, influencing physical health and neurological processes.

Psychological Benefits of Gratitude

At the psychological level, gratitude is consistently associated with greater happiness. Studies show that gratitude helps people feel more positive emotions, relish good experiences, improve their health, deal with adversity, and build strong relationships. One of the landmark studies in this field by Dr. Robert Emmons and Dr. Michael McCullough involved asking participants to write a few sentences each week focusing on particular topics. One group wrote about things they were grateful for during the week, another group wrote about daily irritations or things that had displeased them, and the last group wrote about events that had affected them (with no emphasis on them being positive or negative). After 10 weeks, those who wrote about gratitude were more optimistic and felt better about their lives than the other groups. Surprisingly, they also exercised more and had fewer visits to physicians than those who focused on sources of aggravation.

Gratitude has also been linked with improved mental resilience. Following traumatic events, grateful people recover more quickly. This resilience stems from the role gratitude plays in promoting a positive mindset and an adaptive approach to coping with stress. In the face of life's challenges, grateful individuals tend to appreciate the 'silver linings' and can thus rebound from stressful situations more effectively.

Physiological Effects of Gratitude

On the physiological front, gratitude has been linked with better sleep, reduced stress, and overall improved physical health. A study by Dr. Paul J. Mills of the University of California, San Diego's School of Medicine found that patients who were more grateful actually had better heart health, less inflammation, and healthier heart rhythms. They were also less likely to develop heart disease. The mechanism behind this could be related to the reduction in stress levels that gratitude promotes. Chronic stress is known to worsen health in a myriad of ways, and by alleviating stress, gratitude indirectly contributes to better physical health.

Neurologically, gratitude has profound effects on the brain. Research using functional magnetic resonance imaging (fMRI) has shown that gratitude activates several brain regions associated with the neurotransmitter dopamine, which is known as the 'reward neurotransmitter'. Gratitude can thus enhance dopamine production, which not only makes us feel good but also encourages our brain to seek out more of the same positive activity. It creates a positive feedback loop in our brains, rewarding us for being grateful and driving us to feel and express gratitude more often.

Further, gratitude also influences the hypothalamus, which regulates essential bodily functions such as appetite, sleep, temperature, metabolism, and growth. Another study indicates that the hypothalamus is activated when we feel gratitude, highlighting how deep-seated the effects of gratitude can be on bodily functions.

Gratitude and Social Interaction

Gratitude also plays a critical role in social interactions. It acts as a social glue that binds people together, promoting social cohesion and mutual support. By expressing gratitude, individuals not only acknowledge the role of others in their wellbeing but also foster deeper connections. This is evident in various studies that have examined the role of gratitude in relationships. For example, a study by Sara Algoe from the University of North Carolina at Chapel Hill found that partners who express gratitude to each other are more likely to stay in their relationships, with mutual gratitude being a significant predictor of relationship quality.

Gratitude as a Therapeutic Intervention

Given these benefits, gratitude is increasingly used in therapeutic settings. Cognitive Behavioral Therapy (CBT) and other therapeutic approaches often incorporate gratitude exercises as part of treatment for depression and other mood disorders. These exercises help shift attention from negative or destructive thoughts to more positive, constructive thinking patterns.

The science behind gratitude is robust, spanning from its psychological benefits in enhancing mood and emotional wellbeing, to physiological benefits such as better sleep and reduced symptoms of illness. As we understand more about how gratitude works, it is clear that cultivating an attitude of gratitude can profoundly impact our lives and health in multiple dimensions. This research not only encourages individuals to practice gratitude daily but also highlights its potential as a powerful tool for improving overall wellbeing and happiness.

ᘖᘖᘖ

"When we express gratitude, we open doors to
positive relationships and close the windows to
negativity. Each thank you we utter is not just
courtesy, but a building block for stronger
connections. Let gratitude be the foundation on
which trust and respect are built."

❦❦❦

THREE

STARTING WITH SELF-APPRECIATION

Self-appreciation is an essential aspect of emotional and psychological well-being, serving as the foundation upon which gratitude towards others can be built. It involves recognizing and valuing one's own worth and the positive aspects of oneself, contributing significantly to enhanced self-esteem and overall mental health. Engaging in self-appreciation allows individuals to acknowledge their achievements, embrace their imperfections, and maintain a compassionate attitude towards themselves, which is crucial for personal growth and fulfillment.

The Role of Self-Appreciation in Self-Esteem

Self-esteem is fundamentally about how much we like and appreciate ourselves, regardless of the circumstances we find ourselves in. It reflects a person's overall subjective emotional evaluation of their own worth. Self-appreciation boosts self-esteem by reinforcing the positive aspects of our identity and accomplishments, which in turn cultivates a stronger sense of love and respect for oneself. This positive self-regard is not only about recognizing strengths but also about accepting weaknesses without harsh judgment.

High self-esteem, fostered through self-appreciation, is linked to many benefits such as lower anxiety, resistance to stress and depression, and more successful coping strategies in difficult times. It motivates people to take better care of themselves and pursue their goals with confidence and resilience. Conversely, low self-esteem can lead to negative outcomes such as fear of failure, social anxiety, and a diminished capacity to form secure and honest relationships.

Techniques for Cultivating Self-Appreciation

One effective technique for enhancing self-appreciation is through the practice of positive affirmations. These are positive statements that, when repeated often, can help to change negative thought patterns into positive ones. Affirmations such as "I am worthy of good things," and "I accept myself as I am," can fortify an individual's mindset to appreciate their intrinsic value.

Mindfulness meditation is another powerful practice that enhances self-appreciation. It involves focusing on the present moment while calmly acknowledging and accepting one's feelings, thoughts, and bodily sensations. This practice can help individuals detach from negative self-judgment and develop a greater appreciation of their journey and experiences, regardless of perceived flaws or mistakes.

Journaling is also a beneficial tool for self-appreciation. Keeping a self-appreciation journal where one regularly writes down things they like about themselves or achievements they are proud of can significantly boost self-esteem. This exercise helps to focus the mind on positive attributes and acts as a reminder of an individual's capabilities and worth.

Engaging in self-care activities is a direct expression of self-appreciation. Whether it's taking time to read, enjoying a long bath, engaging in physical exercise, or pursuing a hobby, these activities are ways of honoring the body and mind, affirming that one deserves time and effort.

The Impact of Self-Appreciation on Daily Life

Incorporating self-appreciation into daily life can have transformative effects. When individuals acknowledge their worth, they are more likely to make choices that reflect this positive self-image. For example, they may choose healthier relationships or opt for career paths that align more closely with their values and interests, rather than settling for less fulfilling options.

Moreover, self-appreciation encourages a lifestyle of continual personal development. Recognizing their own value, individuals are more inclined to invest in themselves, seeking out educational opportunities, personal growth experiences, and professional development, which further enhances their life satisfaction and capabilities.

The benefits of self-appreciation also extend into social interactions. Individuals who value themselves are better equipped to foster positive interactions with others. They are less likely to engage in destructive behaviors, such as jealousy or excessive competitiveness, because they feel secure in their own worth. This security allows them to appreciate and celebrate the successes and attributes of others without feeling threatened.

Self-appreciation is a critical component of mental health and well-being, fostering a positive self-image that benefits all areas of life. By practicing techniques such as affirmations, mindfulness, journaling, and self-care, individuals can cultivate a deeper sense of self-appreciation. This internal respect sets the stage for healthier relationships, personal resilience, and a fulfilling life, establishing a stable foundation of self-esteem that supports personal and interpersonal growth. The journey of self-appreciation is not merely about achieving a better state of mind but is also a profound process of recognizing and affirming one's inherent worth and potential.

ᚦᚦᚦ

"The practice of gratitude is not about ignoring
life's challenges but about framing them within a
broader context of appreciation. It allows us to see
the silver linings, teaching us resilience and hope.
Gratitude does not make problems disappear, but it
does reveal the strengths we gain from them."

ppp

FOUR

Expressing Gratitude in Family

Expressing gratitude within the family dynamic is pivotal in strengthening emotional bonds and fostering a nurturing environment that supports mutual respect and love. In the realm of familial relationships, gratitude acts as a powerful connector, easing communication barriers, and enhancing understanding among family members. It serves as an emotional signal that communicates value and respect, contributing to a healthier and more cohesive family unit.

Understanding the Impact of Gratitude in Families

Gratitude in family dynamics can significantly influence the overall emotional climate of the home. Families that regularly express gratitude towards each other tend to experience higher levels of positive emotions and lower levels of negative emotions. This emotional benefit translates into better coping during stress and conflict, improved relationship satisfaction, and a stronger sense of connectedness. Gratitude helps each family member feel valued and appreciated, which is crucial for deepening trust and affection.

Research indicates that expressions of gratitude within a family can lead to members feeling more appreciated and needed, which increases their engagement and satisfaction in family roles. Moreover, gratitude helps buffer against the erosion of relationships over time, which can often occur due to the stresses of daily life or significant life changes such as moves, job changes, or the challenges of raising children.

Practical Tips for Cultivating Gratitude in Family Life

One effective way to cultivate gratitude within a family is through verbal affirmations. Simple statements of appreciation, such as thanking a family member for doing household chores or acknowledging a child's effort in school, can make a significant impact. These acknowledgments should be specific, noting the particular action and its positive impact on the family. For example, a parent might say, "Thank you for setting the table—it made preparing dinner much smoother and reminded me how you contribute to our home's warmth."

Regular family meetings provide another excellent opportunity to foster gratitude. During these gatherings, each member can share something they are grateful for about another family member or a recent family experience. This practice not only allows each person to reflect on positive aspects of family life but also makes it a collective experience, reinforcing the family's identity and unity.

Creating a gratitude board in a common area of the home where family members can post notes of thanks or appreciation for each other is another visual and interactive way to cultivate an attitude of gratitude. This can serve as a constant reminder of the love and appreciation that flows within the family, encouraging a more gracious atmosphere.

Incorporating gratitude into family rituals can also be highly effective. Whether it's saying what you're thankful for during mealtime or having a gratitude moment during family outings or holidays, these practices help normalize expressing gratitude and make it a fundamental part of family life.

The Role of Role Modeling

Parents and caregivers play a crucial role in modeling gratitude. By expressing gratitude themselves, both within and outside the family, adults can demonstrate to children and other family members how to appreciate and recognize the value of others. This modeling can significantly influence children's social and emotional development, teaching them how to express gratitude naturally and authentically.

Furthermore, encouraging acts of kindness and generosity within the family can enhance feelings of gratitude. When family members perform acts of service for one another without being asked, it not only benefits the receiver but also enriches the giver, creating a virtuous cycle of giving and gratitude.

Overcoming Challenges in Expressing Gratitude

Despite its benefits, consistently expressing gratitude in family dynamics can sometimes be challenging. Family life is often hectic, and stress, misunderstandings, and conflicts can overshadow feelings of thankfulness. To overcome these challenges, it is vital to make a conscious effort to maintain a gratitude practice, especially during tough times. This might involve stepping back during conflicts to reflect on what one appreciates about the other person, which can shift perspectives and reduce hostility.

Integrating gratitude into family life is a profound way to enhance relationships, improve emotional health, and create a supportive and loving home environment. By practicing gratitude, families can not only enjoy the immediate benefits of a more harmonious home but also set the foundation for long-term relational success, ensuring that family bonds continue to strengthen and flourish over time. This practice of gratitude, while simple in concept, requires commitment and mindfulness but promises significant rewards for those who make it a central part of their family life.

ᏉᏉᏉ

"A life enriched with gratitude is less likely to be swayed by temporary setbacks. When we cultivate a habit of recognizing good, we equip ourselves with a shield against despair. Gratitude is the armor we wear to guard against life's adversities."

ᐅᐅᐅ

FIVE

BUILDING TRUST THROUGH APPRECIATION

Gratitude is a fundamental element in nurturing and deepening the bonds of romantic relationships. It fosters an environment of mutual respect and appreciation, which are critical for building and sustaining trust between partners. When gratitude is actively practiced in relationships, it not only affirms the value of the partner but also strengthens the relational foundation through enhanced emotional connectivity and trust.

The Role of Gratitude in Romantic Relationships

In romantic relationships, gratitude serves as a key indicator of relationship health and longevity. It acts as an emotional acknowledgment of the partner's value and the contributions they make to the relationship, which in turn reinforces their worth and the commitment to each other. Expressing gratitude towards one's partner can counteract taken-for-grantedness, which often creeps into long-term relationships. Partners who feel valued are more likely to feel satisfied with their relationship and committed to their significant other.

Gratitude also has a unique ability to improve the quality of communication between partners. By focusing on positive attributes and expressing thankfulness, couples can create a more positive interaction pattern, contrasting sharply with interactions characterized by criticism or negativity. This positive communication style makes it easier for both partners to express their needs and concerns openly, knowing that their expressions will likely be met with understanding rather than defensiveness.

Deepening Connections Through Gratitude

One way gratitude deepens connections in romantic relationships is by enhancing emotional intimacy. When partners regularly express gratitude to each other, they reveal a level of vulnerability that can lead to greater intimacy. This expression shows that they do not take each other for granted, fortifying their emotional bond. Studies have found that couples who practice gratitude are more likely to engage in behaviors that promote bonding and are better equipped to deal with relationship conflicts constructively.

Furthermore, gratitude helps to mitigate the impact of negative emotions that can cloud judgment and lead to resentment. It acts as a buffer, offering a wider perspective that helps individuals see beyond temporary issues and appreciate the broader aspects of their relationship. By maintaining a gratitude practice, couples can keep a positive reservoir that they can draw upon during times of conflict or stress.

Practical Ways to Cultivate Gratitude in Romantic Relationships

Cultivating gratitude in romantic relationships can be achieved through various practical and straightforward practices. One effective approach is through daily gratitude rituals. Partners can set aside time each day to share things they appreciate about each other. This could be as simple as thanking each other for everyday actions like making coffee or as significant as expressing appreciation for being supportive during a tough time.

Another method is to keep a couple's gratitude journal. Both partners can contribute entries about what they appreciate about each other and the relationship. Reviewing this journal can be a heartwarming experience, especially during challenging times, as it serves as a reminder of the love and gratitude that exist between them.

Surprise notes of appreciation or unexpected acts of kindness can also be a delightful way to show gratitude. Whether it's leaving a loving note in a partner's bag, sending a thoughtful text during the day, or preparing a favorite meal, these acts of kindness are powerful demonstrations of gratitude and appreciation.

Building Trust Through Appreciative Actions

Trust in romantic relationships is greatly enhanced when partners actively demonstrate their appreciation for each other. Trust builds when one feels secure with their partner, knowing that their contributions are seen and valued. Gratitude reinforces this security by consistently acknowledging and valuing these contributions.

Furthermore, gratitude encourages a positive feedback loop within relationships. When one partner expresses gratitude, the other is more likely to respond positively, which in turn motivates reciprocal expressions of appreciation and acts of kindness. This cycle promotes a growing sense of trust and commitment.

Integrating gratitude into romantic relationships is a powerful strategy for deepening connections and building trust. It transforms the way partners interact with each other, fostering a positive, supportive, and resilient relationship dynamic. By making gratitude a regular practice, couples can enhance not only their relationship satisfaction but also their overall emotional and psychological well-being. This commitment to a grateful outlook helps ensure that the relationship remains strong, flexible, and deeply connected, even as it evolves and faces new challenges over time.

ϷϷϷ

"Gratitude in the workplace does more than create a
pleasant environment; it builds a foundation of
mutual respect and encouragement. By
acknowledging the efforts of others, we not only lift
their spirits but also propel the whole team
forward. Let's create spaces where appreciation
fuels ambition."

♥♥♥

SIX

GRATITUDE IN FRIENDSHIPS

Gratitude plays a crucial role in fostering and maintaining strong friendships. It acts as a reinforcing agent that not only acknowledges the value of a friend's actions but also deepens the emotional bond between individuals. By regularly expressing appreciation, friendships can flourish and withstand the tests of time and conflict, making gratitude a vital component in healthy, lasting relationships.

The Significance of Gratitude in Friendships

In the context of friendships, gratitude serves several important functions. It acknowledges the efforts and qualities of friends, making them feel valued and appreciated. This recognition often leads to increased mutual respect and a stronger, more secure connection. Furthermore, gratitude in friendships promotes a positive interaction cycle. When one friend expresses gratitude, it encourages reciprocal appreciation and kindness, which reinforces the bond and creates a more fulfilling relationship for both parties.

Gratitude also enhances the emotional quality of friendships. It fosters greater joy and satisfaction within the relationship by focusing on positive experiences and attributes. This positive focus helps friends to overlook minor grievances and misunderstandings, prioritizing the good in each other and the relationship. Moreover, grateful people are more likely to be forgiving, which is an essential quality in maintaining long-term friendships that inevitably experience ups and downs.

Deepening Friendships Through Shared Gratitude

One effective way to deepen friendships through gratitude is by making it a regular part of interactions. This could be as simple as expressing thanks when a friend does something helpful or acknowledging a friend's good qualities in conversation. Such expressions of gratitude make friends feel recognized and reinforce their positive behavior, encouraging a healthy dynamic within the friendship.

Another method is through shared experiences that foster gratitude. Participating in activities that both friends are grateful for, such as volunteering, can enhance the sense of camaraderie and shared purpose. These experiences not only provide fun and enjoyment but also create shared memories and stories that further bond friends together.

Gratitude can also be cultivated through mutual support during difficult times. Offering genuine support and expressing appreciation for a friend's presence during a crisis can significantly strengthen the friendship. This reciprocal support not only helps both friends through challenging times but also builds a foundation of trust and gratitude that is priceless in any relationship.

Practical Applications of Gratitude in Friendships

Regularly acknowledging and celebrating the achievements of friends is a practical application of gratitude that can strengthen bonds. Congratulating friends on their successes, whether through a simple message or celebrating together, shows genuine interest and appreciation for their life outside of the friendship.

Keeping a gratitude journal focused on friendships can also be beneficial. Regular entries about what one appreciates in their friends and the positive experiences shared together can increase one's awareness and appreciation of these relationships. Reviewing this journal can be a powerful reminder of the value of each friendship, especially during times of personal doubt or conflict.

Unexpected gestures of appreciation can have a profound impact on friendships. Surprising a friend with a thoughtful gift, a note, or a gesture that says 'I appreciate you' can go a long way in reinforcing the bond. These acts of kindness show that one values the friendship and is willing to put effort into maintaining and enhancing it.

Sustaining Friendships Through Gratitude

Maintaining long-term friendships often requires effort and intentionality, with gratitude acting as a key component of this dynamic. By continually expressing gratitude, friends can avoid taking each other for granted, which is crucial for sustaining the friendship over time. Gratitude keeps the relationship fresh and meaningful, ensuring that both parties feel valued and important.

Gratitude is an essential element in the maintenance and enhancement of friendships. It not only helps individuals connect on a deeper emotional level but also creates a positive feedback loop of kindness and appreciation. By making gratitude a cornerstone of friendships, individuals can enjoy richer, more rewarding relationships that are capable of enduring life's challenges. This practice not only enhances individual lives but also contributes to a more empathetic and connected society.

❥❥❥

"Teaching gratitude to children is planting seeds for a garden of empathy and kindness that will grow throughout their lives. It prepares them to face the world not just with skills, but with hearts full of generosity. Every lesson in gratitude is a lesson in humanity."

❦❦❦

SEVEN

Appreciation in the Workplace

Appreciation in the workplace is a powerful tool that can transform an organization's culture, enhancing employee satisfaction, strengthening team cohesion, and increasing overall productivity. When gratitude becomes a core component of the workplace, it creates an environment where employees feel valued and respected, which in turn motivates them to perform their best work. The strategic implementation of appreciation can foster a positive work environment that benefits both employees and the organization as a whole.

Cultivating a Culture of Gratitude in the Workplace

Creating a culture of gratitude in the workplace begins with leadership. Leaders who express genuine appreciation for their team's efforts set a tone that encourages openness and mutual respect. This leadership by example can significantly influence the entire organizational culture, making gratitude a fundamental part of the company's values.

To effectively cultivate this culture, organizations can implement regular recognition practices that highlight employee achievements. These can range from formal programs, like Employee of the Month awards, to more informal practices, like shout-outs during team meetings or personal thank-you notes from managers to their team members. Such recognition not only boosts the morale of the individual employees but also serves as a model for others to express their gratitude and appreciation.

Implementing Structured Gratitude Practices

Structured gratitude practices can be integrated into the workplace through various programs and initiatives. One effective approach is the creation of a 'kudos' board, where employees can post notes of thanks or recognition for their colleagues. This board acts as a visible reminder of the appreciation flowing within the team and encourages a continuous exchange of gratitude.

Another structured practice is the inclusion of gratitude rounds in meetings, where team members can share what they appreciate about one another or recent team achievements. This practice not only starts meetings on a positive note but also helps in building interpersonal relationships and enhancing team spirit.

Companies can also leverage technology to foster gratitude. Digital platforms where employees can recognize each other's contributions can be particularly effective in large organizations or in remote work settings. These platforms often allow for points or badges to be awarded, which can then be redeemed for rewards, further incentivizing the practice of gratitude.

Gratitude as a Driver for Employee Engagement and Retention

Gratitude in the workplace directly impacts employee engagement and retention. Employees who feel appreciated are more likely to be committed to their organization's goals and are less likely to leave for another job. This sense of appreciation also encourages employees to go above and beyond their regular duties, contributing to a more vibrant and proactive workplace.

In addition to increasing engagement, gratitude helps in building a supportive work environment that can significantly reduce workplace stress and burnout. When employees feel supported by their peers and superiors, they experience lower levels of job-related stress and higher satisfaction with their work-life balance.

Benefits of Gratitude on Team Performance and Collaboration

Gratitude also enhances team performance and collaboration. When team members express appreciation for each other's efforts, it builds a sense of trust and cooperation. This positive team dynamic can lead to improved problem-solving skills and more innovative thinking because team members feel more comfortable voicing their opinions and ideas.

Moreover, gratitude helps in smoothing over workplace conflicts. By fostering an atmosphere where appreciation is regularly expressed, potential tensions can be defused early on. When employees focus on what they appreciate in their colleagues, they are less likely to dwell on minor annoyances or disagreements.

Long-Term Implications of a Grateful Workplace

The long-term implications of fostering a grateful workplace are profound. Organizations that embrace gratitude report higher levels of employee satisfaction, lower turnover rates, and better overall performance. These organizations are often viewed more favorably by outsiders, making them more attractive to top talent and potential business partners.

Integrating gratitude into the workplace is not just about improving employee morale; it is about creating a sustainable and positive work environment that can significantly enhance organizational success. By implementing regular appreciation practices, fostering leadership that values gratitude, and encouraging an atmosphere of mutual respect, companies can reap the benefits of a more motivated, engaged, and cohesive workforce. This investment in gratitude is an investment in the company's future, promising not just happier employees but a more resilient and dynamic organization.

❧❧❧

"In relationships, gratitude acts as the glue that binds and the buffer that protects. It reminds us why we chose each other, even when times get tough. Let your relationships flourish under the nurturing care of appreciation."

♡♡♡

EIGHT

TEACHING CHILDREN THE VALUE OF GRATITUDE

Teaching children the value of gratitude is one of the most profound gifts a caregiver can give. Instilling an attitude of appreciation from an early age can shape a child's worldview, enhancing their ability to enjoy life, empathize with others, and navigate challenges with resilience. By fostering gratitude, parents and educators can contribute to the development of emotionally intelligent, compassionate, and grounded individuals.

The Importance of Gratitude in Early Development

Gratitude is more than just saying thank you. It involves recognizing and appreciating the value of something or someone, which can significantly influence a child's emotional and social development. Children who learn to practice gratitude from an early age develop a sense of abundance and contentment. This outlook helps them appreciate what they have rather than constantly seeking more, fostering a sense of stability and satisfaction.

Moreover, gratitude is closely linked to increased happiness and optimism. Studies have shown that grateful children are happier and more sociable. They show less envy, are more likely to share, and are more resilient in the face of adversity. This resilience is crucial in today's fast-paced, often challenging world, where children who can maintain a positive and grateful mindset are typically better equipped to handle stress and setbacks.

Methods for Instilling Gratitude in Children

One of the most effective ways to teach children gratitude is through modeling. Children learn behaviors by observing and mimicking adults, particularly their parents and teachers. When they see their caregivers expressing gratitude regularly—whether it's thanking someone for a small kindness, showing appreciation for a meal, or expressing gratitude for a sunny day—they begin to understand its value and mimic this behavior.

Incorporating gratitude into daily routines can also reinforce this value. This might involve practices such as discussing things one is grateful for during dinner, encouraging children to thank each other for acts of kindness, or starting a family gratitude journal where everyone can write down or draw things they are thankful for each day. These routines not only help children practice gratitude but also make it a regular part of their lives, enhancing its impact.

Creative activities can further engage children with the concept of gratitude. For example, crafting thank-you cards, creating gratitude collages, or keeping a gratitude jar where they can deposit notes about things they are thankful for are engaging ways that help children express gratitude. These activities make the concept of gratitude tangible and fun, encouraging children to participate enthusiastically.

The Role of Books and Stories in Teaching Gratitude

Books and stories are powerful tools for teaching children about gratitude. Stories that highlight themes of thankfulness, generosity, and appreciation can have a profound impact on a child's understanding of gratitude. Through characters and scenarios, children can see examples of gratitude in action, which can inspire them to act similarly in their own lives. Caregivers can enhance this learning by discussing the stories, focusing on why characters might feel grateful and how expressing gratitude affects those around them.

Encouraging Empathy and Reflective Thinking

Teaching gratitude is also closely tied to fostering empathy. By encouraging children to consider the feelings and perspectives of others, caregivers can help them understand why gratitude is important. Activities like role-playing can help children step into someone else's shoes and appreciate the efforts of others, from the family members who help them with daily tasks to community workers who keep their environment safe and clean.

Reflective thinking is another crucial aspect of teaching gratitude. Encouraging children to think about how different their lives might be without certain people or things can deepen their appreciation for those elements. This reflective practice can be as simple as having conversations about what life would be like without certain comforts or people who make their lives better.

Long-Term Benefits of Gratitude for Children

The long-term benefits of instilling gratitude in children are extensive. Beyond the immediate effects on happiness and social behavior, gratitude can contribute to lifelong wellbeing. It creates a framework through which children—and eventually adults—view the world, which can lead to greater satisfaction and less stress in their lives. Grateful individuals are also more likely to contribute positively to society, showing kindness and support to others, and engaging in community matters with a sense of responsibility and appreciation.

Teaching children the value of gratitude is a vital aspect of their development. By integrating gratitude into everyday practices, using creative methods, and encouraging empathy and reflection, caregivers can lay a strong foundation for children's emotional and social growth. This education in gratitude not only benefits the children themselves but also enriches the communities they belong to, spreading a culture of appreciation and kindness.

ᕦᕦᕦ

"Every act of gratitude is a verse in the poem of kindness we write daily. The more we write, the richer our lives become. Fill your pages with thanks, and read a story of joy and contentment."

♡♡♡

NINE

GRATITUDE IN TIMES OF CONFLICT

Gratitude is a powerful tool in navigating and mitigating conflicts. In situations of disagreement or tension, expressing appreciation can act as a transformative force, helping to diffuse negativity and foster mutual understanding. By acknowledging the value and efforts of others even in challenging times, gratitude can create a bridge towards resolution and harmony.

The Role of Gratitude in Conflict Resolution

Conflict, whether in personal relationships, workplaces, or between communities, often arises from misunderstandings, unmet expectations, or feelings of disregard. Gratitude has the unique ability to shift the focus from what is wrong to what is right, from deficits to contributions. When individuals express appreciation in the midst of conflict, it can change the dynamics of the interaction, softening attitudes and opening the door to constructive communication.

Expressing gratitude during conflicts helps to lower defenses, making individuals more receptive to understanding the perspectives and feelings of others. It signals respect and acknowledgment of the other's value, which can be crucial in tense situations where individuals feel undervalued or unheard. This act of appreciation can thus serve as a powerful antidote to resentment and anger, which are common barriers to conflict resolution.

Practical Ways to Utilize Gratitude in Conflicts

One effective approach to incorporating gratitude in times of conflict is to begin conversations with affirmations or acknowledgments of the positive aspects of the relationship or situation. For instance, starting a difficult conversation with a coworker by acknowledging their hard work or past contributions sets a positive tone and demonstrates respect for their efforts. This can make it easier to address any issues constructively, without triggering defensiveness.

Another strategy is to actively look for and comment on the positive intentions or actions of others, even when disagreements arise. This involves giving the benefit of the doubt and focusing on the potential positives in another person's actions or words. For example, if a partner fails to complete a task, recognizing their other contributions before addressing the oversight can help maintain a positive atmosphere and prevent the conflict from escalating.

Using gratitude to reflect on past resolutions can also be beneficial. Reminding oneself and others of previous times when conflicts were successfully resolved can reinforce a sense of competence and cooperation, encouraging a more optimistic outlook on current disagreements. This reflection can foster a belief in the ability to overcome challenges together, strengthening the relationship and facilitating more effective problem-solving.

The Impact of Gratitude on Emotional and Psychological Well-being in Conflicts

Gratitude not only affects interpersonal dynamics but also has a profound impact on individual emotional and psychological well-being during conflicts. By focusing on gratitude, individuals can experience reduced stress and anxiety, as gratitude naturally counteracts the fight-or-flight response typically triggered by conflict. This shift can lead to clearer thinking and better decision-making, as individuals are less clouded by negative emotions.

Moreover, the practice of gratitude encourages a broader perspective, helping individuals to see beyond the immediate conflict and appreciate the bigger picture. This can reduce the perceived severity of the problem and promote more flexible thinking about potential solutions. Gratitude also builds emotional resilience, empowering individuals to handle conflicts with greater calmness and confidence.

Sustaining Relationships Through Gratitude

Long-term, the regular practice of expressing gratitude in times of conflict can help sustain and deepen relationships. It creates a foundation of positive interactions and memories that can serve as a buffer against future disagreements. Relationships fortified with gratitude are more likely to withstand the strains of conflict because they are rooted in mutual respect and appreciation.

In organizational settings, fostering a culture of gratitude can significantly improve team cohesion and conflict management. When team members regularly acknowledge each other's contributions, they build a reservoir of goodwill that can be crucial in times of stress or disagreement. This culture reduces the frequency and intensity of conflicts and supports quicker, more collaborative resolutions.

Gratitude is an essential tool in conflict resolution, capable of transforming potentially destructive situations into opportunities for growth and understanding. By integrating gratitude into everyday interactions and particularly in times of conflict, individuals and organizations can not only resolve disputes more effectively but also enhance the quality of their relationships and their overall well-being. This approach to conflict, centered around appreciation and understanding, promotes a more compassionate and cohesive social and professional environment.

ᗐᗐᗐ

"Gratitude is the echo of kindness in the heart; it multiplies with each reflection. When given freely, it returns with increased vigor, strengthening the bonds of our interactions. Live a life that echoes gratitude, and kindness will be your reward."

❦❦❦

TEN
CULTIVATING A DAILY GRATITUDE

Cultivating a daily gratitude practice is a simple yet profoundly effective way to enhance one's quality of life. By intentionally focusing on the aspects of life that we are grateful for, we can develop a more positive outlook, increase our happiness, and improve our mental and physical health. Integrating gratitude into daily routines is not just about occasional acknowledgment but about making it a consistent habit that shapes our thoughts and behaviors.

Benefits of a Daily Gratitude Practice

Regular gratitude practice has been shown to have numerous benefits. Psychologically, it can boost mood and resilience against stress. It enhances self-esteem by reducing social comparisons that often lead people to feel resentful towards others who have what they perceive they lack. Instead, by focusing on their own blessings, people are more likely to experience joy and contentment.

Physiologically, practicing gratitude can improve physical health, shown by research to enhance sleep quality, reduce symptoms of physical pain, and increase cardiovascular health. People who engage in regular gratitude practices tend to take better care of their health—they exercise more regularly and are more likely to attend check-ups, which contributes to longevity.

Starting a Gratitude Journal

One of the most straightforward methods to cultivate a daily gratitude practice is to keep a gratitude journal. This involves writing down things you are thankful for each day. These can range from significant events like a job promotion to everyday occurrences like a kind gesture from a stranger. The act of writing helps to solidify these thoughts and make them more concrete. For many, the best time to write in their gratitude journal is at the end of the day, reflecting on the day's events. This not only serves to embed those positive moments into memory but also helps to end the day on a positive note, which can improve sleep.

Gratitude Reminders Throughout the Day

Another effective strategy is to set up gratitude reminders. These can be visual cues placed in the environment—like sticky notes with affirmative messages around your home or workspace, or digital reminders set on your phone. The idea is to have frequent prompts that encourage you to pause and think about something you're grateful for at that moment. This method helps to break the routine of daily life and infuse it with moments of gratitude, which can significantly lift one's spirits and shift one's perspective.

Sharing Gratitude with Others

Sharing feelings of gratitude with others can also be a powerful practice. This could be in the form of sharing what you are grateful for with family members around the dinner table or sending a thank-you note or message to someone who has made a difference in your life. Expressing gratitude to others not only strengthens relationships but also amplifies the positive effects of gratitude by spreading joy and appreciation.

Mindful Appreciation

Mindfulness and gratitude are closely linked—both involve a heightened state of awareness and a focus on the present moment. You can practice mindful appreciation by taking a few moments each day to really focus on something you usually take for granted. This could be a hot shower, the comfort of your bed, the taste of your food, or the beauty of the sky. By fully engaging with these experiences and appreciating their presence in your life, you deepen your gratitude practice and enhance your sensory appreciation of the world around you.

Integrating Gratitude into Existing Routines

For gratitude to become a habit, it needs to be integrated into your daily routines. This can be achieved by attaching gratitude practices to established habits. For instance, while brushing your teeth, think of three things you were grateful for during the day. Or, while waiting for your morning coffee to brew, take the time to feel grateful for the new day ahead. These practices ensure that gratitude becomes a seamless part of your daily life.

Long-Term Commitment to Gratitude

Maintaining a gratitude practice requires a long-term commitment. It's helpful to regularly reflect on the benefits you're experiencing and adjust your practices as needed to keep them fresh and engaging. Over time, gratitude can shift from a practice to a habitual way of experiencing the world, marked by an increased recognition of all there is to be thankful for.

Cultivating a daily gratitude practice is a journey that offers profound rewards. Simple practices like keeping a gratitude journal, setting reminders, sharing gratitude, practicing mindful appreciation, and integrating gratitude into daily routines can transform not just moments of your day, but your entire life outlook. This transformative habit can lead to greater personal happiness, improved health, and stronger relationships, making it a worthwhile investment in your overall well-being.

ᔑᔑᔑ

"The strength of gratitude lies in its ability to illuminate the good in the bad, the happy in the sad. It is a beacon of positivity in a sea of negativity. Hold fast to gratitude, and you will always find your way."

▷▷▷

ELEVEN

THE ART OF SAYING THANK YOU

The simple act of saying "thank you" carries immense power, often underestimated in its ability to transform both everyday interactions and profound relationships. This small but mighty phrase is more than mere politeness; it is a fundamental expression of gratitude that acknowledges the efforts and contributions of others, reinforcing a sense of value and respect that can strengthen bonds and create positive social exchanges.

Understanding the Impact of Saying Thank You

The impact of saying "thank you" extends beyond the immediate moment of exchange. It can deeply affect how people view themselves and their relationships with others. When someone is thanked, they not only feel appreciated but are also more likely to view the thanker as a warmer and more caring individual. This perception can significantly influence the dynamics of both personal and professional relationships, fostering trust and openness.

In the workplace, for example, a culture where thanks are regularly expressed is often one where employees feel more motivated and valued. This can lead to enhanced job satisfaction, greater teamwork, and improved productivity. In personal relationships, expressing thanks can deepen connections, making partners, friends, and family members feel appreciated and cherished.

When to Use Thank You Effectively

While "thank you" is universally beneficial, its effectiveness is magnified when used appropriately and thoughtfully. Recognizing when and how to use this simple expression can make a significant difference in its impact.

After Receiving Help: Whether it's a colleague who assisted with a project or a stranger who held the door open, saying thank you in these instances recognizes the person's effort and kindness.

When Receiving a Gift: This is one of the most common scenarios for saying thank you, but it's important to express genuine appreciation not just for the gift but for the thought behind it.

During Daily Interactions: Regularly expressing gratitude for the small things people do every day, such as a family member making dinner or a friend sending a supportive text, can reinforce relationships and create a positive atmosphere.

In Professional Settings: Thanking a mentor for their guidance or a team member for their hard work is crucial in maintaining respectful and mutually beneficial professional relationships.

In Response to Kindness: Whenever someone extends kindness, no matter how small, acknowledging it with a thank you can encourage more positive behavior and spread goodwill.

How to Say Thank You Effectively

The effectiveness of a thank you also depends on how it is delivered. The following strategies can enhance the sincerity and impact of your gratitude:

Be Specific: Instead of a generic thank you, be specific about what you are thankful for. For instance, "Thank you for spending the afternoon helping me with the report. Your expertise really made a difference," shows appreciation not just for the help but for the individual's unique contribution.

Personalize Your Gratitude: Personalizing your thanks can make it more meaningful. A handwritten thank you note or a thank you gift that suits the recipient's interests can leave a lasting impression.

Use Eye Contact: When possible, say thank you while making eye contact. This nonverbal cue reinforces sincerity and connection.

Follow Up: If someone has gone out of their way to assist you, follow up with them later to let them know the outcome and reiterate your thanks. This shows that their help was valuable and had a positive impact.

The Long-Term Benefits of Practicing the Art of Saying Thank You

Regularly practicing the art of saying thank you can have profound long-term benefits. It cultivates an environment of mutual respect and appreciation, which are cornerstone qualities of successful and enduring relationships. In the workplace, it can transform the organizational culture, creating a more positive and collaborative atmosphere. In personal life, it enhances bonds and contributes to a supportive, loving environment.

Furthermore, the practice of saying thank you is beneficial for the one expressing gratitude as well. It encourages a mindset of noticing and appreciating the good in life, which can enhance psychological wellbeing and happiness. People who frequently express gratitude are generally more positive, happier, and more satisfied with their lives.

The art of saying thank you is a simple yet powerful tool that can significantly influence personal, social, and professional interactions. By acknowledging the efforts and kindness of others with a sincere thank you, individuals foster an atmosphere of respect and appreciation that enriches their relationships and enhances their own sense of well-being. This simple act, when practiced regularly, can transform not just moments, but entire relationships, making it a critical element of successful interpersonal interactions and a fulfilling life.

ϷϷϷ

"Gratitude is the lens that focuses on what is right, not what is lacking. Through this lens, we see the world in its true splendor. Adjust your focus and discover the abundance that surrounds you."

❥❥❥

TWELVE

USING TECHNOLOGY TO FOSTER GRATITUDE

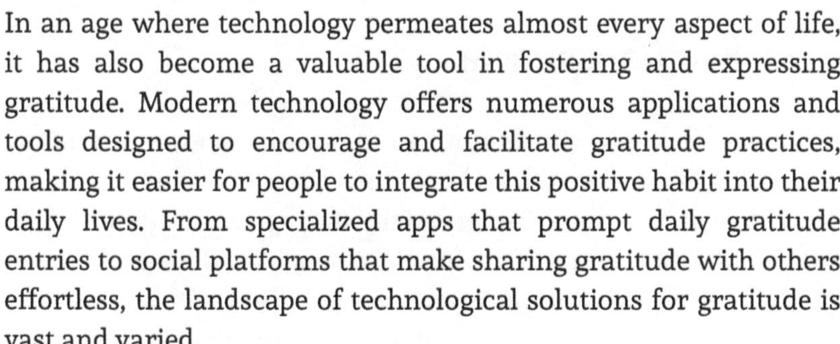

In an age where technology permeates almost every aspect of life, it has also become a valuable tool in fostering and expressing gratitude. Modern technology offers numerous applications and tools designed to encourage and facilitate gratitude practices, making it easier for people to integrate this positive habit into their daily lives. From specialized apps that prompt daily gratitude entries to social platforms that make sharing gratitude with others effortless, the landscape of technological solutions for gratitude is vast and varied.

Gratitude Apps

Several apps are dedicated to helping individuals cultivate gratitude. These apps often include features like daily reminders to enter things you're grateful for, prompts to inspire thoughts of gratitude, and the ability to look back on past entries. This digital journaling can significantly enhance a person's consistency in practicing gratitude, offering a convenient and accessible platform for reflection.

Gratitude Journal Apps: Apps like *Grateful* and *Day One* allow users to maintain a digital gratitude journal. These apps often offer customization options such as adding photos or other media to gratitude entries, which can enhance the personal connection to the memories and items listed.

Reminder-Based Apps: Apps such as *Thankful* provide daily reminders to users to log moments of gratitude. They might also include features like inspirational quotes or daily challenges that encourage deeper reflection and appreciation for life's many gifts.

Community-Based Apps: Platforms like *Happier* provide a community aspect where users can share their gratitude entries with others. This can help foster a sense of connection and shared joy, further enhancing the benefits of gratitude practices.

Social Media and Online Platforms

Social media can be a powerful tool for spreading gratitude. Many people use platforms like Facebook, Instagram, and Twitter to share what they are thankful for, especially during certain times of the year like Thanksgiving, or for specific campaigns like the 30 days of gratitude challenge. Sharing gratitude publicly can not only amplify personal feelings of gratitude but also inspire others to reflect on what they are grateful for in their own lives.

Blogging: Personal blogs or community blogging sites like *Medium* offer spaces for longer-form gratitude posts, where individuals can share detailed stories and accounts of their gratitude experiences. This can serve as a source of inspiration and encouragement for both the writer and their readers.

Video Sharing Platforms: Video platforms like YouTube are excellent for sharing gratitude stories or creating gratitude-focused content, such as daily or weekly gratitude vlogs. These videos can be a more personal and engaging way to connect with others over shared grateful experiences.

Technological Integration in Daily Life

Technology can also integrate gratitude practices into daily life through more subtle means.

Smart Home Devices: Devices like Amazon Echo or Google Home can be programmed to remind you to reflect on what you're grateful for at certain times of the day, integrating gratitude seamlessly into your daily routine.

Fitness Trackers and Smartwatches: Devices like Fitbit or Apple Watch can send reminders or allow you to set custom notifications to pause and consider moments of gratitude throughout the day, tying in well-being with physical health monitoring.

Desktop and Browser Apps: Tools like *Momentum* on Chrome offer a new tab page that features a daily quote and a prompt for gratitude, turning a routine act of opening a new browser tab into a moment of reflection.

Challenges and Games

Technology also enables unique ways to engage with gratitude through challenges and gamification.

Gratitude Challenges: Apps and platforms often host challenges such as a "21-day gratitude challenge" to encourage users to practice gratitude more consistently and make it a habit.

Gamified Apps: Some apps use gamification to encourage gratitude practices by awarding badges, streaks, or levels as users consistently log their gratitude, making the process fun and engaging.

Technology offers diverse and innovative tools that can significantly support and enhance the practice of gratitude. Whether through apps designed specifically for gratitude journaling, social media platforms that facilitate sharing and community building, or everyday technologies that remind us to pause and reflect, these tools can help embed gratitude more deeply into our daily lives. By leveraging technology, individuals can maintain a consistent practice of gratitude, enhancing their mental and emotional well-being and fostering a more positive and appreciative outlook on life.

ppp

"In moments of gratitude, time pauses, and the heart understands what truly matters. These moments build a life of deep satisfaction and purpose. Cherish them, nurture them, and watch your life align with your deepest values."

ppp

THIRTEEN

APPRECIATION ACROSS CULTURES

Gratitude is a universal human emotion, but the ways in which it is expressed can vary significantly across different cultures. Understanding these differences can enrich our own practices of gratitude and appreciation, offering us a broader perspective on how to acknowledge the positive aspects of life. By exploring how various cultures express gratitude, we can learn to appreciate the diversity of gratitude practices and the underlying values that guide them.

Gratitude in Eastern Cultures

In many Eastern cultures, gratitude is often expressed through actions rather than words. In Japan, for example, the act of giving and receiving is surrounded by rituals that emphasize respect and appreciation. The presentation of a gift is just as important as the gift itself, often accompanied by a bow to show respect and gratitude. Japanese culture also emphasizes the importance of 'on,' a deep sense of indebtedness to others, which is a fundamental part of social interactions. This indebtedness is not seen as a burden but as a valuable connection that enhances the social fabric.

In India, gratitude is deeply intertwined with spiritual and religious practices. Offering thanks to the gods through rituals and prayers is a common way to express gratitude. Additionally, the act of sharing, especially food, is a significant expression of gratitude and hospitality in Indian culture. This not only shows appreciation for the guests but also for the bounty that life has provided, creating a cycle of giving and receiving that reinforces community and family bonds.

Gratitude in Western Cultures

In Western cultures, particularly in the United States, gratitude is frequently vocalized and encouraged as an individual emotion. Phrases like "thank you" are common in everyday interactions, reflecting a culture that values acknowledgment of individual contributions and kindness. The celebration of Thanksgiving is a notable example of a culturally embedded practice of gratitude, where people reflect on and express thanks for the past year's blessings.

European expressions of gratitude often combine both verbal thanks and gestures. In France, for instance, saying "merci" is almost reflexive in social interactions, and is often supplemented with phrases that emphasize the gratitude, such as "merci beaucoup" (thank you very much). In many European cultures, sending thank you cards or flowers after receiving a gift or being hosted for a meal is a common practice, showing appreciation through both words and gestures.

Gratitude in Indigenous Cultures

Indigenous cultures around the world often embody gratitude in their everyday lives and spiritual practices in profound ways. For many Native American communities, gratitude is a central theme, expressed through rituals and ceremonies that honor the Earth and its resources. The concept of giving thanks is an integral part of daily life, seen as vital to maintaining balance and harmony within the community and the natural world.

In these communities, gratitude is not only directed at people but also at the natural world, acknowledging and respecting the symbiotic relationships that sustain life. Ceremonies such as the Potlatch among the Indigenous peoples of the Pacific Northwest involve elaborate gift-giving and feasting, which are expressions of wealth redistribution and gratitude among community members.

Learning from Global Gratitude Practices

By examining the ways in which different cultures express gratitude, we can gain insights into the values they hold sacred. Eastern practices teach us the value of integrating gratitude into our social fabric through actions and rituals that emphasize respect and indebtedness. Western practices highlight the importance of acknowledging individual acts of kindness and the benefits of institutionalizing gratitude in celebrations.

Indigenous practices remind us of the deeper connections between gratitude, community, and the environment, suggesting that our expressions of thanks should extend beyond the human sphere to include the natural world that supports us.

In today's globalized world, embracing diverse gratitude practices can enhance our understanding of human relationships and the many ways we can express appreciation. It encourages us to be more mindful and intentional in how we express gratitude, and to recognize the profound impact our thanks can have on strengthening bonds and promoting a more compassionate and interconnected world.

Exploring how different cultures express gratitude not only

broadens our understanding of this universal emotion but also enriches our own practices. By learning from each other, we can cultivate a deeper and more inclusive approach to gratitude, enhancing our relationships and contributing to a more harmonious global community. This cultural exchange of gratitude practices offers valuable lessons on respect, generosity, and the importance of community, providing us with diverse ways to appreciate and celebrate the many gifts of life.

ϷϷϷ

"A simple 'thank you' can travel miles and bridge
distances, connecting hearts in unexpected ways.
Never underestimate the power of gratitude to
change a day, or even a life. Let gratitude travel
freely, spreading joy wherever it goes."

♡♡♡

FOURTEEN

OVERCOMING BARRIERS TO GRATITUDE

Gratitude is widely recognized for its positive effects on both individual well-being and interpersonal relationships. However, cultivating a consistent attitude of gratitude can sometimes be challenging due to various psychological, social, and cultural barriers. Understanding these challenges and learning how to overcome them is essential for anyone looking to deepen their practice of gratitude and enjoy its many benefits.

Identifying Common Barriers to Gratitude

One of the primary challenges to feeling and expressing gratitude is the human tendency to adapt to positive life circumstances—a phenomenon known as hedonic adaptation. Over time, people tend to take for granted the good things in their lives, whether it's a job promotion, a loving relationship, or material comforts. This adaptation can diminish the intensity with which we feel and express gratitude.

Another significant barrier is envy or jealousy, which can skew perception and focus one's attention on what others have that one does not. This comparison can lead to feelings of inadequacy or resentment, both of which are antithetical to gratitude.

Negative bias, which is the tendency to pay more attention to negative events than positive ones, also poses a substantial challenge. This evolutionary trait can make it difficult to notice or remember positive events or gestures, thereby reducing opportunities to feel grateful.

Strategies to Overcome These Barriers

1. Practicing Mindfulness: Mindfulness involves staying present and fully experiencing the moment without judgment. By practicing mindfulness, individuals can become more aware of their everyday experiences and the numerous opportunities for gratitude that they might otherwise overlook. Mindfulness meditation can help recalibrate attention towards the positive, countering the effects of negative bias and promoting a greater appreciation for small, everyday blessings.

2. Keeping a Gratitude Journal: One effective way to combat hedonic adaptation is by keeping a gratitude journal. Regularly writing down things one is grateful for can help individuals notice and appreciate the good in their lives more consistently. This practice can also serve as a valuable record to look back on during tougher times, providing a reminder of positive aspects that one might currently overlook.

3. Changing Comparison Habits: To counteract feelings of envy or jealousy, it can be helpful to consciously change one's comparison habits. Instead of comparing oneself with those perceived to have more, individuals can try to compare down—considering those in less fortunate situations. This perspective can foster feelings of gratitude for one's own circumstances. Moreover, shifting focus from comparison to compassion can lead to a more gratitude-centered outlook.

4. Gratitude Prompts: For those who struggle with remembering to acknowledge what they're thankful for, setting daily gratitude prompts can be beneficial. Whether it's an alarm on one's phone or a sticky note on the bathroom mirror, these reminders can help integrate gratitude more deeply into daily routines.

5. Expressing Gratitude Out Loud: Verbally expressing gratitude can reinforce feelings of appreciation and make them more tangible. Making it a habit to thank others, whether for significant gestures or everyday kindnesses, can enhance one's awareness of others' contributions to their well-being and strengthen interpersonal connections.

6. Reflecting on Obstacles Overcome: Reflecting on past difficulties and acknowledging how one has grown or what one has learned from them can cultivate a sense of gratefulness for the present. This reflection can shift the focus from what one lacks to the strengths and new opportunities that past challenges have fostered.

Creating a Culture of Gratitude:

Beyond individual practices, fostering a culture of gratitude within one's family, workplace, or community can help sustain gratitude practices. When groups of people collectively engage in expressing appreciation, it creates a positive feedback loop that encourages continual acknowledgment and appreciation.

Long-term Commitment to Gratitude:

Finally, it is important to view gratitude as a long-term commitment rather than a one-time fix. Regularly revisiting and adjusting one's gratitude practices can keep them fresh and responsive to one's evolving life circumstances and challenges. As with any habit, consistency is key, and the more ingrained these practices become, the more natural expressing gratitude will feel.

While there are numerous barriers that can impede our ability to feel and express gratitude, there are just as many effective strategies to overcome these obstacles. By incorporating practices such as mindfulness, gratitude journaling, and deliberate expression of thanks into daily life, individuals can enhance their capacity to appreciate and enjoy the positive aspects of their lives and relationships. This not only enriches one's own life experience but also contributes to creating a more empathetic and appreciative community.

ppp

"Gratitude is not a finite resource but a renewable
energy that grows with each expression. The more
you use it, the more powerful it becomes. Tap into
this energy, and let it light up your life."

♡♡♡

FIFTEEN

GRATITUDE IN THE COMMUNITY

Gratitude can transform not just individual lives but also the communities in which people live. When gratitude is practiced on a communal scale, it fosters a supportive, positive, and interconnected environment. Communities characterized by a culture of gratitude experience stronger bonds among members, reduced conflicts, and a greater willingness to participate in communal activities or aid one another. Therefore, actively spreading and encouraging gratitude within a community can have profound effects on its overall health and happiness.

Promoting Gratitude Through Community Events

One effective way to foster gratitude within a community is through organized events that celebrate and encourage thankful expression. Events such as community appreciation days or gratitude-themed gatherings can provide platforms for members to express thanks to each other and to recognize valuable contributions within the community. These events can be tailored to highlight specific groups such as volunteers, educators, public service workers, or residents who go above and beyond to help others in their local area.

Community Service and Volunteerism

Participating in or organizing community service activities is another powerful way to cultivate gratitude. Volunteerism not only aids those in need but also instills a sense of gratitude in volunteers themselves. By contributing to the betterment of their community, individuals often gain a deeper appreciation for their own circumstances and develop a greater awareness of the positive impact they can have. Organizing regular community clean-ups, food drives, or support groups encourages ongoing engagement and fosters a grateful and cooperative spirit among participants.

Gratitude Projects and Initiatives

Communities can initiate projects specifically designed to spread gratitude. For example, creating a "Wall of Gratitude" where community members can post notes expressing their thanks for others in the community can be a visually impactful and engaging way to promote grateful sentiments. Similarly, a community gratitude journal, available in public places like libraries or community centers, can serve as a collective record of the community's grateful thoughts and experiences.

Educational Workshops and Programs

Offering workshops or programs that educate community members about the benefits of gratitude and ways to integrate it into their daily lives can also be beneficial. These can include sessions led by psychologists or community leaders, focusing on the practical applications of gratitude in personal and social contexts. Schools can incorporate gratitude into their curricula, teaching students from a young age the importance of being thankful and recognizing the efforts of others.

Recognition and Rewards Programs

Implementing recognition and rewards programs can motivate community members to express gratitude and engage in helpful behaviors. These programs can highlight acts of kindness and gratitude, rewarding them with community acknowledgments, certificates, or small prizes. This not only celebrates those who contribute positively but also sets a public example, encouraging others to act similarly.

Utilizing Local Media

Local media, whether online platforms, community radio stations, or newspapers, can play a crucial role in fostering a culture of gratitude. Regular features that focus on stories of gratitude, kindness, and community support can help shift the communal focus towards positivity and appreciation. These stories can inspire others and create a ripple effect, multiplying the impact of a single grateful act.

Building Partnerships Among Local Businesses

Encouraging local businesses to participate in community gratitude efforts can amplify the effects. Businesses can sponsor gratitude events, offer special rewards for community volunteers, or participate in community service projects. This not only helps spread gratitude but also strengthens the bonds between local businesses and the community, creating a network of mutual support and appreciation.

Creating a Sustainable Culture of Gratitude

For gratitude to have a lasting impact on a community, it must be sustained beyond occasional initiatives. This requires ongoing effort and creativity in keeping the community engaged. Regular meetings, continuous opportunities for community involvement, and consistent messages of gratitude through various channels can help maintain momentum. Encouraging leaders within the community to model gratitude and making gratitude practices a part of community tradition can anchor these values deeply within the local culture.

Spreading and encouraging gratitude within a community can significantly enhance the social fabric of the area. By organizing community events, fostering volunteerism, initiating gratitude projects, and utilizing local media, communities can build an environment where gratitude flourishes. Such efforts not only improve the immediate social environment but also contribute to the long-term well-being and resilience of the community, making it a more supportive and connected place for everyone.

ϟϟϟ

"Living gratefully is an art that colors every day with joy and every interaction with warmth. It teaches us that each person we meet is a gift, and every moment shared is a treasure. Paint your life with gratitude, and it will be a masterpiece."

♡♡♡

SIXTEEN

THE LONG-TERM BENEFITS OF LIVING

Living a life filled with gratitude can have profound long-term benefits on an individual's health, happiness, and overall well-being. Cultivating an attitude of gratitude transforms not just fleeting moments of joy, but shapes life trajectories, influencing everything from psychological health to physical well-being and interpersonal relationships. Understanding and embracing these benefits can motivate a consistent practice of gratitude, leading to a more fulfilling and resilient life.

Psychological Benefits of Gratitude

One of the most significant impacts of living gratefully is on mental health. Numerous studies have demonstrated that gratitude can decrease symptoms of depression and anxiety. By focusing on what is positive in their lives, individuals can shift away from negative thought patterns that are often associated with these mental health challenges. Gratitude enhances mood by releasing dopamine and serotonin, two neurotransmitters responsible for our emotions and feelings of happiness and well-being.

Gratitude also increases psychological resilience, making

individuals better equipped to handle the stresses of daily life. It fosters a stronger sense of personal worth and can buffer against trauma's negative effects by promoting positive coping strategies. People who practice gratitude consistently report fewer feelings of helplessness or overwhelming negativity when faced with adversity. Instead, they are more likely to approach challenging situations with a mindset that appreciates potential growth and learning opportunities.

Physical Health Improvements

Living gratefully also benefits physical health. Studies have found that individuals who engage in regular gratitude practices report fewer physical symptoms, such as pain and fatigue, and demonstrate better immune function. They often experience lower blood pressure and are less likely to develop chronic diseases such as hypertension or heart disease. This could be partly attributed to the role of gratitude in reducing stress and anxiety, which are known contributors to a variety of physical health issues.

Moreover, grateful people tend to engage in healthier behaviors and self-care practices. They are more likely to exercise regularly and make healthier food choices. They also show a greater propensity to seek help for health concerns and adhere to medical advice, leading to better management of chronic conditions and overall greater longevity.

Enhanced Sleep Quality

Another key benefit of living a life of gratitude is improved sleep. Practicing gratitude can help calm the mind and reduce the anxious or racing thoughts that often lead to insomnia. Regularly writing in a gratitude journal, for instance, has been shown to positively influence sleep patterns. Individuals who jot down what they are thankful for before bed tend to fall asleep faster and experience better quality sleep throughout the night.

Strengthened Relationships

Gratitude has a remarkable ability to enhance relationships. When individuals express gratitude towards their friends, family, or partners, it fosters a greater sense of connection and satisfaction within those relationships. This expression of appreciation makes others feel valued and helps to build trust and reciprocal respect. Over time, this strengthens relational bonds and can make personal interactions more fulfilling and supportive.

Moreover, gratitude can increase social support, which is crucial for long-term well-being. Feeling grateful can make people more likely to seek out and maintain supportive relationships and less likely to feel lonely or isolated. In communities, gratitude can contribute to a more cooperative and generous atmosphere, enhancing social networks that are essential during times of need.

Emotional and Social Well-being

Gratitude enriches emotional life not only by increasing positive feelings like joy and contentment but also by reducing the prevalence and intensity of negative emotions such as envy, resentment, and regret. A grateful disposition encourages a focus on what one has, rather than what one lacks, leading to greater emotional complexity that can better navigate the ups and downs of life.

Socially, gratitude can lead to increased generosity and empathy. Recognizing and appreciating what others have done for them makes people more likely to pay it forward. This creates a cycle of kindness and appreciation that can ripple throughout a community, improving social bonds and making collective social environments more nurturing.

The long-term benefits of living a life of gratitude are extensive and impactful. From significantly improving mental and physical health to enhancing interpersonal relationships and social well-being, gratitude can fundamentally alter life experiences for the better. By incorporating gratitude into daily life and recognizing its transformative potential, individuals can enjoy not only greater happiness and health but also a deeper, more meaningful existence. This lifelong practice is not merely about feeling better in the short term but about fostering enduring health, happiness, and harmony.

ϸϸϸ

"Gratitude does not change the scenery; it enhances
the view. It allows us to see the extraordinary in the
ordinary, the remarkable in the routine. Change
your perspective with gratitude, and watch your
world change."

ᐅᐅᐅ

SEVENTEEN

Gratitude is a transformative force that can profoundly impact individuals and relationships in remarkable ways. Real-life stories and case studies of people who have embraced gratitude provide compelling evidence of its power to change lives. These narratives not only inspire but also offer practical insights into how adopting a grateful mindset can lead to significant improvements in well-being, happiness, and interpersonal connections. Here are several case studies that illustrate the transformative effects of gratitude.

Case Study 1: Overcoming Personal Loss

The first case involves Sarah, a middle-aged woman who experienced the devastating loss of her spouse. Grief overwhelmed her daily life, leading to depression and isolation. As part of her therapy, Sarah was encouraged to start a gratitude journal. Initially skeptical, she began noting small things she was grateful for—supportive friends, a caring family, and even her pet's companionship.

Over time, Sarah noticed a shift in her perspective. Focusing on gratitude helped her appreciate the network of support she had and the good memories she shared with her spouse, rather than solely mourning his absence. This practice didn't eliminate her grief but provided a way to balance her loss with an appreciation for life's continuing blessings. Eventually, Sarah reported feeling more connected to others and found renewed motivation to engage in activities that brought her joy.

Case Study 2: Transforming a Strained Parent-Child Relationship

The second story focuses on Michael, a father struggling with his teenage daughter, Emily's rebellious behavior. Resentment and anger had replaced the close bond they once shared. During a family counseling session, the therapist introduced the concept of expressing gratitude to each other daily, regardless of ongoing tensions.

Michael and Emily started leaving gratitude notes for each other, acknowledging anything from chores completed to aspects of each other's character they admired. This practice slowly improved their communication, helping both to see each other's efforts and good qualities rather than just the points of conflict. Over several months, gratitude helped restore a sense of appreciation and love between them, dramatically improving their relationship.

Case Study 3: Enhancing Workplace Morale and Productivity

A small tech startup faced high employee turnover and low morale. The CEO, recognizing the need for a more positive work environment, implemented a "Gratitude Wall" where employees could post notes of thanks or recognition for their colleagues' hard work and support.

This initiative changed the workplace atmosphere. Employees began to feel more valued and saw their contributions acknowledged. Not only did this boost individual morale, but it also enhanced team cohesion and collective problem-solving abilities. The company noted improved employee retention and increased productivity as team members became more engaged and cooperative, feeling that their efforts were genuinely appreciated.

Case Study 4: Health Recovery and Gratitude

Another profound example involves Linda, who was undergoing treatment for breast cancer. Throughout her treatment, Linda maintained a gratitude blog, where she documented her journey and expressed thanks for the support from healthcare professionals, family, and friends. She also wrote about her gratitude for life's everyday joys, even on difficult days.

Linda's focus on gratitude provided her with a psychological buffer against the physical and emotional toll of cancer treatment. Her doctors reported that her positive attitude played a crucial role in her recovery process. Moreover, her blog became a source of inspiration and support for other patients facing similar challenges, expanding the ripple effect of her gratitude.

Case Study 5: Recovery from Financial Hardship Through Gratitude

Finally, consider the case of Tom, who faced significant financial difficulties after a business failure. The stress led to despair and strained family relationships. At a workshop, Tom learned about the role of gratitude in enhancing resilience and perspective. He began to practice daily gratitude, acknowledging his family's support, the lessons learned from business challenges, and even his remaining business contacts.

This shift in focus led to new approaches in managing his finances and rebuilding his business. Gratitude helped Tom remain optimistic and open to new opportunities, eventually leading to the recovery of his financial stability. His family relationships also improved as he frequently expressed his appreciation for their patience and support.

These case studies illustrate the diverse and powerful ways in which gratitude can transform lives. From personal loss to professional environments, the practice of gratitude provides individuals with tools to enhance resilience, improve relationships, and maintain a positive outlook through various life challenges. By learning from these real-life examples, others can be inspired to incorporate gratitude into their own lives, potentially leading to profound personal and relational transformations.

ᗡᗡᗡ

"The echoes of gratitude resonate well beyond the initial word or gesture. They build a legacy of positivity that can transform communities and inspire generations. Start small, think big, and create a legacy of gratitude."

❦❦❦

EIGHTEEN

Gratitude and Mental Health

Gratitude is more than a simple thank-you; it's a transformative practice that can have significant positive impacts on mental health. Over the past few decades, psychological research has increasingly focused on how gratitude interventions can alleviate symptoms of mental illness and enhance overall psychological well-being. These interventions, ranging from journaling to therapy-based exercises, harness the power of gratitude to shift focus from negative to positive aspects of life, reinforcing feelings of contentment and satisfaction.

Understanding the Psychological Impact of Gratitude

Gratitude has been linked to a variety of mental health benefits, including reduced symptoms of depression and anxiety, enhanced resilience, and greater overall happiness. One reason for these benefits is that gratitude helps individuals to contextualize and reframe their experiences more positively. By focusing on what they are thankful for, people can shift their attention away from toxic emotions such as envy, resentment, or regret. This shift can significantly decrease the mental load associated with negative thinking, which is often a driving factor in mood disorders like depression.

Another way in which gratitude improves mental health is by enhancing social support, which is a critical factor in protecting against psychological disorders. People who practice gratitude regularly are often more empathetic and supportive, qualities that make them both good companions and recipients of social support. The reciprocal nature of social interactions fueled by gratitude can create a supportive network that fosters both giving and receiving support, buffering against the loneliness and isolation that often accompany mental health issues.

Gratitude Interventions in Therapy

In therapeutic settings, gratitude interventions are often employed to help clients focus on positive experiences and foster feelings of thankfulness, even in difficult circumstances. These interventions can vary but typically include several key practices:

Gratitude Journaling: One of the most common and effective gratitude interventions is keeping a gratitude journal. Clients are encouraged to write down things they are grateful for on a daily basis. This practice can help shift attention from negative or obsessive thoughts to a more balanced perspective that acknowledges the good alongside the bad.

Gratitude Visits: This involves writing and delivering a letter of thanks to someone who has had a positive impact on one's life but has not been properly thanked. The exercise provides both the writer and recipient with a profound emotional experience, often bringing to light the positive influences that go unrecognized.

Gratitude Meditation: Focusing meditation on feelings of gratitude towards oneself or others can enhance the emotional and psychological benefits of regular meditation practices. This type of meditation often involves visualizing the faces of loved ones and mentally offering them thanks, which can significantly boost one's mood and sense of connection.

Research Findings on Gratitude and Mental Health

Empirical studies provide robust evidence supporting the efficacy of gratitude practices in improving mental health. For example, research has shown that individuals who engage in gratitude journaling report lower levels of depression and stress, and they feel happier and more satisfied with their lives. Similarly, studies on gratitude visits have found that participants experience significant increases in happiness and significant decreases in depressive symptoms, often lasting for months after the intervention.

Moreover, gratitude can counteract the symptoms of serious psychological disorders. For instance, in patients with anxiety or depression, gratitude exercises can decrease symptom severity and enhance coping efficacy. Gratitude's positive effects also extend to lessening the experience of pain in individuals with physical health conditions, illustrating its broad therapeutic impact.

Long-Term Benefits of Gratitude for Mental Health

The long-term benefits of regular gratitude practice include sustained improvements in mood and emotional well-being. By continuously engaging in gratitude practices, individuals can develop a more optimistic outlook on life, better stress management skills, and increased emotional resilience. These benefits, in turn, contribute to better mental health outcomes over time.

Furthermore, gratitude can enhance self-esteem by reducing social comparisons that often lead to feelings of inadequacy. By appreciating their own life and achievements without comparing them to those of others, individuals can enjoy improvements in self-worth and self-satisfaction.

Gratitude interventions offer a powerful tool for enhancing mental health and well-being. Whether incorporated into daily personal routines or formal therapeutic settings, gratitude practices can help mitigate the symptoms of psychological disorders, enhance emotional resilience, and foster a deeper sense of happiness and satisfaction in life. By adopting a more grateful outlook, individuals not only improve their own mental health but also contribute to a more positive and supportive environment around them.

❧❧❧

"Each grateful thought is like a note in a symphony
of positivity. Together, they create a melody that
uplifts the soul and harmonizes life's complexities.
Tune your life to the rhythm of gratitude and dance
to its uplifting beat."

❥❥❥

NINETEEN

CREATING YOUR GRATITUDE VISION BOARD

A gratitude vision board is a creative and effective way to visually capture and remind oneself of the things one is grateful for. It serves as a daily reminder of life's positives, reinforcing a mindset of appreciation and contentment. The process of creating a gratitude vision board can be deeply reflective and therapeutic, helping to highlight and prioritize personal values and aspirations. This guide will explore the steps involved in creating a gratitude vision board and discuss how this tool can enhance your awareness and practice of gratitude.

What is a Gratitude Vision Board?

A gratitude vision board is a physical or digital collage of images, quotes, and items that visually represent the aspects of your life that you are thankful for. Unlike traditional vision boards that may focus on future goals and aspirations, gratitude vision boards center around appreciating what is currently present in your life. This could include people, experiences, achievements, or personal strengths. The board acts as a focal point for your gratitude, providing a constant reminder of the good surrounding you.

Benefits of a Gratitude Vision Board

Creating and using a gratitude vision board has numerous benefits:

Enhances Positive Focus: Regularly seeing a visual representation of all you are grateful for helps to shift your focus from what is lacking to what is abundant in your life.

Boosts Mood: The process of creating the board and viewing it can evoke positive emotions and improve your mood.

Increases Satisfaction: Reflecting on the aspects of your life that you value can increase your overall life satisfaction.

Encourages Mindfulness: Engaging with your board can serve as a form of mindfulness practice, where you are fully present in acknowledging the positives in your life.

Steps to Create a Gratitude Vision Board

Gather Supplies If you are making a physical board, you will need a poster board or large piece of paper, magazines, printed images, markers, glue, scissors, and any other craft supplies you might want to use. For a digital board, software like Canva, Pinterest, or even a document editor like Microsoft PowerPoint can be used.

Reflect on What You're Grateful For Before you start creating, spend some time reflecting on what you are truly grateful for. Consider categories such as family, friends, career, personal growth, health, experiences, and material comforts. Make a list of specific items under each category.

Collect Visual Representations For each item on your list, find a visual representation. This could be a photo, a magazine cutout, a meaningful quote, or even a symbol that best captures the essence of what you're thankful for.

Arrange Your Materials Start placing your visuals on your board. There's no right or wrong way to arrange them, but you might like to group similar items together or place the most significant items in the center. Play around with the layout until you feel it best reflects your feelings of gratitude.

Assemble the Board Once you are happy with the layout, begin gluing or pinning your items onto the board. For a digital board, you can simply drag and drop your images into your chosen software and arrange them as you like.

Display Your Board Place your gratitude vision board in a location where you will see it often, such as your bedroom, home office, or another personal space. If it's digital, set it as your desktop wallpaper or as a recurring reminder to revisit it.

Incorporating the Vision Board into Daily Life

To maximize the benefits of your gratitude vision board, make it a part of your daily routine:

Daily Reflections: Spend a few minutes each day looking at your board. You might choose to do this during a morning routine, as it can set a positive tone for the day.

Meditation Focus: Use your board as a focus during meditation, allowing yourself to deeply feel gratitude for each item represented.

Update Regularly: As your life evolves, so too will the things you're grateful for. Periodically updating your board to reflect new blessings keeps the practice relevant and engaging.

A gratitude vision board is a powerful tool to cultivate and maintain a positive and grateful mindset. By visually representing the elements of your life that bring you joy and satisfaction, you create a personal artifact that not only beautifies your space but also deepens your daily practice of gratitude. This process of selecting, creating, and reflecting is itself a practice in mindfulness and appreciation, providing lasting benefits to your mental and emotional well-being.

ᗪᗪᗪ

"Gratitude is the silent music between souls, a melody that needs no words yet feels deeply profound. It's the music that plays quietly but resonates deeply within the heart. Listen closely, and let gratitude's music guide you."

♡♡♡

TWENTY

THE JOURNEY AHEAD WITH GRATITUDE

As we draw near the end of this exploration into the profound impact of gratitude on our lives, it becomes clear that the journey with gratitude does not end here; rather, it is an ongoing process that enriches one's life continuously. The principles and practices shared throughout this book are not just theoretical concepts but are meant to be woven into the fabric of daily living, transforming routine experiences into a deeper, more meaningful engagement with life.

The Everlasting Impact of Gratitude

Living a life filled with gratitude is akin to constantly tending a garden. It is an active, ongoing process that requires attention and care, but the rewards are bountiful. By choosing gratitude, you enrich not only your own life but also the lives of those around you. It enhances relationships, strengthens emotional resilience, and creates a positive feedback loop in social interactions. Over time, this leads to communities where kindness, appreciation, and mutual respect are the norm rather than the exception.

Cultivating a Habit of Gratitude

The cultivation of gratitude as a daily habit can be the single most important change you introduce to your life. Like any habit, it requires commitment and consistency. Whether it's through keeping a gratitude journal, making mental acknowledgments of gratitude daily, or setting aside moments each week to reflect on what you are thankful for, the key is regular practice. These moments of gratitude, though small, accumulate to foster a general attitude of appreciation and positivity that can withstand the challenges and vicissitudes of life.

The Ripple Effects of Gratitude

The practice of gratitude does not exist in a vacuum. Its effects ripple outwards, influencing others' lives and the broader community. When you express gratitude, you not only uplift yourself but also encourage others to pause and reflect on their own lives. This can create a culture of gratitude where the focus shifts from what is lacking to what is abundant. Such a cultural shift can mitigate the harshness of modern life, which often emphasizes achievement and material gain over community and well-being.

Encouraging Gratitude through Teaching and Sharing

One of the most effective ways to deepen your own gratitude is to teach it to others. Sharing the concept of gratitude with family, friends, or through community groups can reinforce your own practice and help others discover its benefits. This could be as formal as leading a workshop or as informal as discussing gratitude practices over coffee. Teaching gratitude not only spreads its benefits but also provides you with new insights and perspectives on your own practices.

Gratitude as a Lifelong Learning Process

Gratitude is not something one masters; it is a lifelong learning process. As you grow and face different stages and challenges in life, your understanding of gratitude can evolve. This dynamic process means that there is always something new to learn and appreciate, keeping the practice of gratitude fresh and relevant. Regularly revisiting your gratitude practices, adapting them to new life circumstances, and exploring new gratitude exercises can keep your practice vibrant.

Challenges and Overcoming Them

It's important to acknowledge that maintaining a gratitude practice isn't always easy. Life's difficulties can sometimes overshadow our ability to feel thankful. During these times, it's crucial to gently remind yourself of the benefits of gratitude and to reach out to others for support. Remember, gratitude is not about ignoring the negative aspects of life but about offering a perspective that balances those difficulties with an awareness of the good.

Looking Forward

As you move forward from this book, carry with you the understanding that gratitude is more than just a tool for happiness. It is a way of seeing the world, a lens that changes not only how you view life but also how you participate in it. It is about living fully, embracing the moment, and appreciating both the highs and the lows. The journey ahead with gratitude is promising and exciting. It holds the potential not just for transformed lives but for a transformed world.

Continue to cultivate gratitude daily. Let it be your companion in moments of joy and your consolation in times of sorrow. Let it guide you to deeper relationships and richer experiences. The journey ahead is bright with the promise of gratitude, and every step taken in gratitude is a step toward a fuller, more joyful life. This is not just the end of a book, but the beginning of a more grateful way of living.

"By nurturing gratitude, we cultivate a garden where kindness and contentment bloom. Each thank you plants a seed, and every act of appreciation waters these seeds. Watch your garden flourish and share its bounty generously."

❥❥❥

TWENTY-ONE
SUMMARY

As we reflect on the themes and insights presented throughout this exploration of gratitude, it becomes evident that gratitude is more than just an emotion—it is a transformative force that can profoundly impact our lives, relationships, and communities. This summary encapsulates the core concepts discussed in each chapter, offering a holistic view of the power and practice of gratitude.

1. The Essence of Gratitude Understanding gratitude begins with recognizing it as an acknowledgment of the goodness in our lives. By focusing on what we have, rather than what we lack, gratitude shifts our perspective towards abundance and positivity, fostering a deeper appreciation for life's gifts.

2. Gratitude and Well-being Gratitude significantly enhances psychological and physiological well-being. It reduces stress, improves mental resilience, and promotes happiness. Physiologically, gratitude can improve heart health, reduce symptoms of illness, and enhance sleep quality, illustrating its broad benefits for physical health.

3. Cultivating Self-Appreciation Gratitude starts with appreciating oneself. Self-appreciation fosters self-esteem and personal growth by encouraging individuals to acknowledge their own strengths and accomplishments. This foundation supports greater confidence and self-compassion, which are crucial for overall well-being.

4. Gratitude in Relationships In the realm of personal relationships, gratitude acts as a crucial bonding agent. Expressing gratitude to family, friends, and partners strengthens connections and fosters mutual respect and affection. It encourages reciprocity and deepens trust, enhancing the quality of these relationships.

5. Gratitude in the Workplace In professional environments, gratitude can lead to better teamwork, increased employee satisfaction, and higher productivity. Creating a culture of appreciation in the workplace fosters a positive work environment and encourages employees to engage more fully with their work.

6. Gratitude and Childhood Development Teaching children the value of gratitude equips them with a tool for emotional resilience and happiness. Gratitude enhances empathy and fosters positive social behaviors, helping children build stronger relationships and better cope with adversity.

7. Gratitude During Challenges Even in times of conflict or difficulty, gratitude has the power to transform negative situations into opportunities for growth and reconciliation. It provides a perspective that can diffuse conflict and foster an environment of cooperation and understanding.

8. Daily Gratitude Practices Incorporating gratitude into daily routines can stabilize and prolong its positive effects. Practices such as gratitude journaling, meditation, or simply pausing to acknowledge life's blessings can reinforce a habit of gratitude.

9. Appreciating Cultural Diversity Exploring how different cultures express gratitude enriches our understanding and appreciation of its universal value. This diversity reveals the many ways gratitude can be woven into the fabric of daily life across the globe.

10. Overcoming Barriers to Gratitude While the practice of gratitude offers numerous benefits, it also faces challenges such as hedonic adaptation and the human tendency to focus on the negative. Overcoming these barriers requires mindfulness, persistence, and creativity in one's gratitude practice.

11. The Art of Saying Thank You A simple "thank you" can have profound implications for interpersonal interactions. This act of acknowledgment can change the dynamics of a relationship, promoting positive communication and mutual respect.

12. Technological Aids Modern technology offers tools that can facilitate and enhance the practice of gratitude. From apps that prompt reflective journaling to social media platforms that allow for the sharing of gratitude, technology can be a valuable ally in cultivating gratitude.

13. Gratitude Across the Lifespan From children to the elderly, gratitude positively impacts individuals at all stages of life. It enhances life satisfaction, emotional well-being, and social integration, proving to be a valuable practice throughout one's life journey.

14. Gratitude as a Community Value When communities embrace gratitude, they see stronger social bonds, increased cooperation, and a more supportive social environment. Community-wide practices of gratitude can transform public spaces into more welcoming and positive places.

15. Long-Term Benefits of Gratitude The long-term practice of gratitude can lead to lasting changes in how individuals experience and interact with the world. It promotes a sustainable lifestyle marked by greater contentment, stronger relationships, and a pervasive sense of joy and satisfaction.

16. Real-Life Gratitude Transformations Through case studies and personal narratives, the impact of gratitude is vividly illustrated in the lives of individuals who have embraced its practice. These stories highlight the profound changes that can occur in personal health, professional environments, and interpersonal relationships.

17. Gratitude and Mental Health Gratitude interventions have proven effective in improving mental health by reducing symptoms of psychological disorders and enhancing emotional resilience. Therapeutic practices that incorporate gratitude can lead to significant improvements in mental well-being.

18. Creating a Gratitude Vision Board A practical application of gratitude, vision boards can help individuals visualize and focus on the aspects of their lives for which they are grateful. This creative expression supports a more focused and sustained gratitude practice.

19. The Journey Ahead with Gratitude Looking forward, the practice of gratitude holds the promise of a richer, more fulfilling life. It is a journey that requires commitment and perseverance but offers invaluable rewards in happiness, health, and harmonious relationships.

Embracing a life of gratitude is not merely about acknowledging the good but about creating a paradigm shift in how we perceive and interact with the world. As we continue beyond this book, let gratitude be your guide to a more joyful and meaningful existence.

❧❧❧

Citation And References

This book represents the culmination of extensive research and meticulous analysis, incorporating a diverse range of sources, including numerous books, scholarly studies, and personal experiences. Additionally, I have scoured various websites to gather relevant information and data essential for the compilation of this work. I have taken every precaution to ensure the accuracy of the information presented and have diligently cited all sources to acknowledge their contributions.

Despite these efforts, the possibility of inadvertent errors remains. I deeply value the insights of my readers and appreciate any feedback that can help identify and rectify such inaccuracies. I encourage you to bring any discrepancies to my attention.

Your feedback is not only welcome but crucial, as it will aid in correcting current editions and enhancing the content of future ones. I am committed to maintaining the highest standards of accuracy and reliability in my work and thank you for your support and understanding.

Additionally, I firmly uphold the principle of freedom of speech and expression as guaranteed under Article 19(1)(a) of the Constitution of India, and I respect the diverse viewpoints and expressions of all readers.

ppp

Other Books Of The Author

1. Empowering Minds: A Journey into Women's Self-Discovery and Power
2. The Dynamics of Motivation: Catalyzing Thought into Action
3. Meditation and Mental Well Being: The Path to Inner Peace and Clarity
4. The Psychology of Child Education: Nurturing Future Generations
5. Ethical Enlightenment: A Modern Guide to Living with Integrity
6. Voices of Empowerment: Stories of Women Rising Against Odds
7. Social Psychology in Everyday Life: Understanding Human Connections
8. The Essence of Motivational Speaking: Inspiring Change in Others
9. Balancing Acts: Women, Work, and the Will to Lead
10. Guiding with Grace: Raising Children with Compassion and Awareness
11. The Power of Positive Aging: Embracing Life After Fifty
12. Building Resilient Communities: Social Work in Action
13. The Ethical Educator: Principles for Teaching and Learning
14. From Insight to Impact: Social Psychology for a Better World
15. The Ethics of Empathy: A Guide to Ethical Living
16. The Science of Empowering the Self: Navigating Life's Challenges with Psychological Wisdom
17. The Mindful Conscious Leader: Meditation Techniques for Modern Management
18. Pioneering Spirit: Women's Pathways to Leadership and Empowerment
19. Feeling to Healing: The Role of Emotional Intelligence in Child Development
20. Transformative Talks and Words of Inspiration: Insights into Motivational Oratory

21. The Hidden Path to Ethical Sustainability: Crafting a Greener Tomorrow
22. Spiritual Integrity: Navigating Life with Moral Compassion
23. Clean Living, Clean Society: The Ethics of Cleanliness
24. Patriotic Spirits: Building a Nation on Positive Attitudes
25. Innovative Integrity & Vibrant Visions: The Ethical and Entrepreneurial Spirit of Gujarat
26. Youthful Visions, Endless Possibilities: Inspiring Ethics and Motivation in Children
27. Living Your Legacy: How to Motivate Others by Living Your Values
28. Secret of Healing Conversations: Ethical Practices in Counselling and Therapy
29. Creative Kindness: Crafting a Life of Compassion and Creativity
30. The Power of Appreciation: How Gratitude Can Transform Your Relationships
31. Bhagavad-Gita: Messages
32. Science of Art: The New Frontier of Fashion Modernism
33. Vivekananda's Virtues: A Blueprint for Modern Living
34. Empower Her: Navigating the Path to Women's Entrepreneurship
35. The Boundless Classroom: Innovations in Global Education
36. The Language of Leadership: Communicating with Authenticity and Impact
37. The Warrior's Mantra: Deciphering the Hanuman Chalisa
38. Echoes of Empathy: Transformative Stories of Social Service
39. Artful Living: Cultivating Creativity in Your Daily Routine
40. Finding Your Why: Discovering Your Passions and Charting Your Course
41. The Role of Social Media in Shaping Self-Esteem and Interpersonal Relationships among Adolescents

ৡৡৡ

Contact

Dr. Minakshi Bansal
Social Activist
Ahmedabad, Gujarat, Bharat
minakshiindiag20@yahoo.com

❥❥❥

|| LOKAHA SAMASTHAHA SUKHINO BHAVANTU ||

• 131 •

www.ingramcontent.com/pod-product-compliance
Lightning Source LLC
Chambersburg PA
CBHW020838120726
48008CB00001B/16

979889415086 4